EXPLORING WORLD CULTURES

Russia

Kaitlyn Duling

Cavendish
Square

New York

Published in 2019 by Cavendish Square Publishing, LLC
243 5th Avenue, Suite 136, New York, NY 10016

First Edition

Website: cavendishsq.com

This publication represents the opinions and views of the author based on his or her personal experience, knowledge, and research. The information in this book serves as a general guide only. The author and publisher have used their best efforts in preparing this book and disclaim liability rising directly or indirectly from the use and application of this book.

All websites were available and accurate when this book was sent to press.

Library of Congress Cataloging-in-Publication Data

Names: Duling, Kaitlyn, author.
Title: Russia / Kaitlyn Duling.
Description: First edition. | New York : Cavendish Square, [2018] | Series:
Exploring world cultures | Includes bibliographical references and index.
| Audience: Grades 2-5.
Identifiers: LCCN 2017048053 (print) | LCCN 2018000000 (ebook) | ISBN
9781502638137 (ebook) | ISBN 9781502638106 (library bound) | ISBN
9781502638113 (pbk.) | ISBN 9781502638120 (6 pack)
Subjects: LCSH: Russia (Federation)--Juvenile literature.
Classification: LCC DK510.23 (ebook) | LCC DK510.23 .D58 2018 (print) | DDC
947--dc23
LC record available at https://lccn.loc.gov/2017048053

Editorial Director: David McNamara
Editor: Jodyanne Benson
Copy Editor: Rebecca Rohan
Associate Art Director: Amy Greenan
Designer: Christina Shults
Production Coordinator: Karol Szymczuk
Photo Research: J8 Media

The photographs in this book are used by permission and through the courtesy of:
Cover Artyom Geodakyan/TASS/Alamy Stock Photo; p. 5 Popova Valeriya/Shutterstock.com; p. 6 Dikobraziy/Shutterstock.com; p. 7 Elena Liseykina/Moment/Getty Images; p. 8 Leemage/UIG/Getty Images; p. 9 Allan Jackson/Getty Images; p. 10 Alexei Nikolsky/TASS/Getty Images; p. 11 Alexei Fateev/Alamy Stock Photo; p. 12 Leonid Ikan/Shutterstock.com; p. 13 Artem Sam/iStock/Thinkstock.comp. 14 Pavel L Photo and Video/Shutterstock.com; p. 15 Ondrej Prosicky/Shutterstock.com; p. 16 Sefa Karacan/Anadolu Agency/Getty Images; p 18 Iakov Filimonov/Alamy Stock Photo; p. 19, 27 ITARTASS Photo Agency/Alamy Stock Photo; p. 20 Kosorukov Dmitry/Shutterstock.com; p. 21 Vlad J55/Shutterstock.com; p. 22 Andrey Kekyalyaynen/Alamy Stock Photo; p. 24 Sharon Vos-Arnold/Moment/Getty Images; p. 26 Yegor Aleyev/TASS/Getty Images; p. 27 Narinder Nanu/AFP/Getty Images; p. 28 Iuliia Kochenkova/Shutterstock.com;
p. 29 Jack F/Fotosearch LBRF/AGE Fotostock.

Printed in the United States of America

Contents

Introduction

Welcome to Russia! Russia's official name is the Russian Federation. This is the largest country in the world. It has over 144 million people! There are cities. There are large rural areas. It stretches across Europe and Asia. It touches several oceans.

Russia has a long history. So much has happened! You might hear about Russia on the news. Russia and the United States also have a long history. It is complex. It is always changing. Over the years, the way of life for Russians has become more like the American way of life. Russian children aren't so different from us.

Russia has an active government. It is also full of culture. It is full of good food. It is both hot and cold. Of course, it is diverse. Russia is huge! Are you ready to learn more? Let's explore this amazing country!

St. Basil's Cathedral was built in the mid-1500s.

Geography

Russia isn't just big. It is the biggest country in the world! In fact, one-tenth of all land on Earth is in Russia. It touches three oceans. It touches the Atlantic. It touches the Pacific. It touches the Arctic, too.

This map shows Russia. Look how large it is!

Russia has many features. It has mountains. It has plains and rivers. Its Ural Mountains divide

FACT!

Over 60 percent of Russia is **taiga**, or forests. This climate is harsh. Summers are short. Winter is very cold.

One of the largest parts of Russia is the **steppe**. This is a huge part of Europe and Asia. It stretches far. The steppe is made of grassland. Some parts are very hot in the summer. Other parts are cold. There are very few trees.

Europe and Asia. It has over 100,000 rivers. It also has an Arctic region. Grasslands and forests are there. Some parts of Russia are dry. They almost feel like desert areas. It even has two of Europe's largest lakes: Ladoga and Onega.

The Altay Mountains sit above the flat steppe.

Russia has an interesting history! People settled there hundreds of years ago. At first, it was divided into small parts. The first **tsar** came to power in the 1550s. He brought the country together.

The Soviet Union was created by Vladimir Lenin.

In 1917, the people took control. They had power over the country. They elected their leaders. It was the first time the people had power. Then, a **communist** group came to power. They were called the Bolsheviks. Vladimir Lenin created the Soviet Union. It was officially known as the Union of Soviet Socialist Republics (USSR). It included

Russia. It had eleven other countries too. The USSR lasted until 1991. Today, we call the entire area Russia.

Russia and America worked together during World War II.

Brrr ... the Cold War

In the 1970s and 1980s, the United States and the USSR had some problems. No shots were fired. No bombs were dropped. This is why it was called a "cold" war. It ended in 1991. The Soviet Union broke up.

VOTE

The Russian government has gone through many changes. For decades, it was part of the USSR. In 1991, the Soviet Union ended. Then Russia held a free election. Boris Yeltsin won. He became president. In 1993, the country wrote its own Constitution.

Russian president Vladimir Putin has served for decades.

In 1999, Yeltsin appointed Vladimir Putin as the prime minister. Putin took over as president

FACT!

Vladimir Putin is one of the world's most powerful leaders.

States? No, Supers

Russia doesn't have states like the United States does. It has seven super regions. Each of those regions has a super governor. This system started in 2000. The regions are South, Central, Northwest, Far East, Siberia, Ural, Volga, and North.

after Yeltsin left. He became president in 2000. He remains president today. The president still chooses the prime minister. In the federal government, there are many agencies and ministries. It is a busy place.

Government headquarters are in Moscow.

11

The Economy

Russia has a mixed economy. This means that the economy is made up of both businesses and the government. For many years, it had an economy in which the government controlled everything. Today, it is more like the United States.

Drills like these bring valuable oil up from the ground.

The country is full of resources. It is especially rich in oil and gas. Other countries use these for

FACT!

Oil and gas make up over 70 percent of Russian **exports**. Exports are things sold to other countries.

Cash Money in Russia

In Russia, people don't pay with dollar bills. They use a currency called the **ruble**. The Bank of Russia began in 1991. The ruble has always been the main type of money.

Russian rubles come in a rainbow of colors!

energy. It also has gold and aluminum. Its arms industry is large. Guns, jets, submarines, ships, missiles, and more are made in Russia. Many Russians work in technology, too. Most of the well-paying jobs are in Moscow. That is the capital of Russia and the largest city.

The Environment

Russia is full of parks, animals, and wild places. However, for many years the Russian government did not watch pollution. Today, the environment is stressed. Many trees have been cut down by loggers. The forests are not protected. Illegal logging is an issue, as are wildfires.

Nuclear power plants cause pollution in Russia.

FACT!

About 1 percent of Russia's land is protected. The areas are called preserves or *zapovedniks*.

Animals in Danger

Many rare animals live in Russia. Bears, polar bears, Siberian tigers, and snow leopards all live there. Unfortunately, many of the animals are endangered. As forests disappear and people hunt illegally, there are fewer tigers and other wildlife.

Water and air pollution are serious problems. These are caused by factories and industry. The use of fossil fuels causes pollution. Oil is a fossil fuel. Pollution causes health problems. The environment is also affected by nuclear power.

The Siberian tiger is the world's largest cat.

The People Today

Russia is home to over 144 million people. It is the largest country in the world. But it does not have the highest population. In fact, it is hardly populated. Many parts of Russia have very few people. Most of the people live in cities where they also work.

Young people in Russia like to have fun with their friends!

Almost three-fourths of Russia's population is **urban,** or living in cities. The rest live in rural areas.

Tatars

Nearly six million people living in Russia identify as Tatars. Historically, they come from early nomadic groups. Many are native to Crimea and the Volga region. There are many forms of the Tatar language.

Most people identify as ethnically Russian. Other groups include Tatars, Ukrainians, Armenians, and many others. Russia also allows many legal immigrants each year, especially Uzbeks and Armenians. There are over one hundred small ethnic groups in Russia. For many decades, the overall population was on the decline. But in recent years, Russia's population has been growing.

Lifestyle

Children in Russia are not so different from you! They go to school. They love to play and learn. Children usually live at home with their parents and siblings. They might live in an apartment. Even though these homes are small, grandparents might live there too. Housing is expensive in Russian cities.

Russian families love spending time together.

FACT!

In addition to roads and rails, Russia also has the world's largest oil pipeline. It carries oil about 2,500 miles (4,023 kilometers).

18

Grandma might help with cooking and cleaning. Dad will probably go to work. Mom might work too. School is very important to Russians. Children go to preschool and advance through the grades. Graduation is a big celebration! College is important. Not all Russians go to college, but many do.

Reading and education are very important to the people of Russia.

Get Going!

Russians have many options when traveling. There are roads and cars, of course. There is also a huge train system. It is nearly as big as the rail system in the United States. You can even ride the train into another country! There are buses and airplanes, too.

Religion

People in Russia have a variety of beliefs. The most popular religion is Russian Orthodox. Around half of Russians consider themselves Orthodox. The church has existed for centuries. It plays a huge role in Russian culture, history, and even government. There are also a few Catholic and other Christian churches in Russia. Islam is the

Most Orthodox churches have large, domed roofs.

FACT!

Russian Orthodox churches are beautiful and intricate. There are over five thousand Russian Orthodox churches in Russia today.

Religious Freedom

Over the last few decades, freedom of religion has become an issue in Russia. Other countries have criticized Russia for its lack of tolerance for other churches and faiths.

second most popular religion in Russia. Tartars, Chechens, and other groups practice Islam. Muslim groups vary.

An Orthodox church is very intricate and richly decorated.

Native faiths have long histories. Their histories stretch back to ancestral groups who lived in present-day Russia long ago. Sometimes this is called "Tengrism" or **shamanic** religion. There are also Buddhists, Hindus, and Jewish groups in Russia, though they are small populations.

21

Language

The only official language of Russia is Russian. When children go to school, they learn Russian. However, today there are over one hundred different languages spoken across the country! Different languages are spoken by

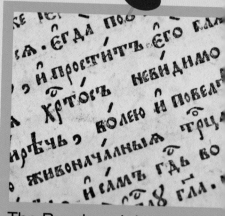

The Russian alphabet has thirty-three letters and look very unique.

migrants. These are people who come from other countries. Many migrants are from countries that were part of the USSR.

Some Russians know foreign languages. English, German, and French are the most popular. Young people who live in big cities often

Can you believe it? Russian is the second-most-used language on the internet, after English.

learn English. In school, the top three languages are taught. Some students also learn Spanish, Chinese, or Arabic. Tatar and Chechen are sometimes taught as well.

The Russian Language

When you travel, you are bound to meet someone who speaks Russian. It is the eighth-most-spoken language in the world! It is the official language in several countries, including Belarus, Kazakhstan, and Kyrgyzstan.

Russians love the arts. The country is full of writers and artists. It has a long history of arts and culture. In fact, some of the world's most famous and respected writers came from Russia. Russian writers wrote novels, plays, and

Nesting dolls are painted in this traditional style.

poetry. Visual art is also important in Russia. Architecture in the country is beautiful. Crafts are also very popular. One of the most notable Russian crafts is the matryoshka, or nesting doll. These are wooden figures that hold other smaller figures.

FACT!

After the end of the USSR, other cultures began to have an influence on Russia. Today, there are even Russian rock and roll bands!

Painters have also enjoyed a long history in Russia. Landscapes, Soviet art, and portraits have been popular at different times. Religious paintings are also an important part of the Russian art culture.

Ballet

Russia doesn't just have artists and writers. It has dancers, too. Russian ballet has been popular since the 1700s. Many famous ballerinas came from Russia. The ballet school and theater in Moscow remains well-known across the globe.

Fun and Play

There is much fun to be had when you live in Russia. Sports are very popular, especially soccer. In other parts of the world, this is called "football." Russia has its own professional football league, as well as a national team. Russians also enjoy ice hockey. They have

Adults and children love to play ice hockey.

won the World Championships more than once. In Russia, there is a game called "bandy" that

FACT!

Have you heard of beach soccer? Russian beach soccer teams tend to win when they play against other countries.

combines soccer and ice hockey. It is similar to ice hockey, but teams play with a ball. It is a traditional Russian sport. Each year, Russia sends athletes to the Olympics for many different sports.

In addition to athletics, Russians are also interested in chess and other games. The video game Tetris was invented in Russia. Tag, cards, and traditional games like P'yanitsa and Wizards are very popular with children.

Video games have grown in popularity.

A Day for Kids

In Russia, there is an entire day devoted to kids! It's called Children's Day. This holiday is celebrated on the first of June.

Food

Since Russia is so big, it is full of different kinds of food. There are some foods that have always been important to Russians. One of these is soup. Some soups are served

A stack of delicate blini is a delicious sight to see!

hot while others are purposely served cold. One of the most well-known cold soups is borscht. It is made with beets, vegetables, and beef.

For breakfast, Russians often eat porridge. This can be made with milk and different grains.

FACT!

Many special desserts and breads are made for the Russian Orthodox Easter holiday.

Food and Drink

Russian cuisine features many delicious baked goods. Stuffed buns are popular. They are often stuffed with meat, vegetables, and eggs. There are also many types of Russian cake. Have you ever tried a blini? They are thin Russian pancakes.

At a Russian meal, you would also find cabbage, onions, and other pickled vegetables. Pickling helps veggies stay edible during the cold months.

A big meal marks Shrovetide, the days before Lent.

Glossary

communist   A way of organizing society in which property and resources are owned by the government.

export   A good that is sold to another country.

migrant   A person who moves from place to place in order to find work.

ruble   The monetary unit of Russia.

shamanic   A spiritual tradition that focuses on nature and creation.

steppe   Flat, treeless grasslands.

taiga   Swampy, forested areas in the high north.

tsar   A Russian leader prior to the early 1900s.

urban   Relating to cities.

Find Out More

Books

Kudela, Katy R. *My First Book of Russian Words*.

Mankato, MN: Capstone Publishing, 2011.

Moon, Walt K. *Let's Explore Russia*. Minneapolis,

MN: Lerner Publishing, 2017.

Website

Kids from Russia

https://www.factmonster.com/people/kids-around-

world/kids-russia

Video

Russia: Winter

https://www.youtube.com/watch?v=eQq3N860gtQ

Index

About the Author

Kaitlyn Duling believes in the power of words to change hearts, minds, and, ultimately, actions. A poet, non-fiction author, and grant writer who grew up in Illinois, she now resides in Pittsburgh, Pennsylvania. She loves to learn about other cultures and go on adventures around the globe.

2983